FELICIA CARTRIGHT

AND THE
GREEN MEDALLION

Felicia   Joan

FELICIA CARTRIGHT

AND THE
GREEN MEDALLION

BERNARD PALMER

ANEKO
PRESS

Aneko Press *Youth*

www.anekopress.com

Aneko Press, Life Sentence Publishing, and our logos are trademarks of
Life Sentence Publishing, Inc.
203 E. Birch Street
P.O. Box 652
Abbotsford, WI 54405

JUVENILE FICTION / Religious / Christian / Action & Adventure

Paperback ISBN: 979-8-88936-286-9

eBook ISBN: 979-8-88936-287-6

10   9   8   7   6   5   4   3   2   1

Available where books are sold

CONTENTS

CHAPTER 1

UPSETTING NEWS

Felicia Cartright pushed her books aside and moved to the window to look out across the campus of the Wellington School for Girls. It had grown colder during late afternoon and was beginning to snow again. Soft white flakes floated downward, etched sharply against the black of night as they sifted into the faint yellow sphere of the streetlight. A car crept over the icy streets and stopped to discharge its passengers at the entrance to the Administration Building, which also doubled as a dorm.

Felicia glanced at the clock on the dresser. Almost time for dinner. She ran her fingers over her soft blond hair, patting the curls into place. She was not a tall girl nor strikingly beautiful. But something about her was distinctive. She was long remembered by those who met her. Her face had a sweet, wholesome quality, and her eyes danced vivaciously, reflecting the smile that was on her lips or lurked, warm and friendly, just beneath the surface.

The door opened and her roommate, Joan Bailey, came bouncing in.

"I thought you were coming up to cram for that history quiz tomorrow, Joan," Felicia said reproachfully.

"So did I." Joan dropped to an easy chair across the room and smiled pleasantly. "But I went for a walk in the snow. It's beautiful out tonight, Felicia."

"I know."

"Besides, I don't feel like studying."

Felicia looked at her, shaking her head. "Do you ever feel like studying, Joan?"

She sat up straight.

"Now you sound like Miss Duncan. You want to watch it, Felicia. You'll be old before your time."

"If I am, it will likely be from worry over you."

"But I'll study for that test after dinner. Honestly I will."

She glanced at the clock again and went to get her coat.

"Did you stop by to see if Sylvia wants to walk to the dining hall with us?"

Sylvia Reynolds was the new girl who came to Wellington on a scholarship at the beginning of the term. A charming girl and a brilliant student, but so shy she had kept to her room except for meals and classes until Felicia and Joan took her in hand.

"I stopped," Joan answered. "I wanted to talk with you about her. Did you look in on her this afternoon?"

"No," Felicia said, pointedly, "I had some studying to do."

"I stuck my head in her room a minute ago. Her eyes were red and swollen, and she looked as though she had been crying for a week."

Felicia was instantly serious. "I saw her at noon, and she was all right."

"So did I." Joan got to her feet and slipped into her coat. "But she's far from all right now."

"You go on to dinner, Joan. I'm going in and talk to Sylvia."

Joan laid a hand on her arm. "I wouldn't if I were you. She acted to me as though she wanted to be alone."

Felicia was silent for a moment.

"She's been so happy lately. Something must be terribly wrong."

While they were standing there, someone knocked at the door. Joan opened it to see the girl who worked in the office.

"Miss Duncan would like to speak with both of you downstairs right away," she said crisply.

"Thank you," Felicia acknowledged.

Joan's face blanched.

"Have you got all your subjects up, Felicia?" she asked.

"As far as I know." The Cartright girl started toward the door, but Joan just stood there.

"I can't understand it," she said. "I made up all my back assignments last week, and you checked them for me."

Her roommate smiled.

"Wouldn't it be a little easier to study than to worry this way?" she asked.

"When something like this comes up, yes," Joan said. "But the trouble is that there are always so many things that are more interesting to do."

They went past Sylvia Reynolds' room at the end of the corridor and down a flight of stairs to Miss Duncan's office. The austere Dean of Wellington was sitting behind her desk. She looked up as they entered.

"Good evening, Felicia and Joan," she said, a smile lighting briefly on her lips.

"Miss Shaffer said that you wished to speak to us."

"Quite right," she said, nodding. "Would you please close the door, Felicia. This conversation must be in the strictest confidence."

"I made up my work in English, Miss Duncan," Joan blurted, "and I have time this evening to study for that history quiz tomorrow. I–"

"You must have a guilty conscience, Joan," Miss Duncan replied mirthlessly. "I didn't call you in to talk with you about your appalling study habits. We have gone over them at length, repeatedly. Won't you be seated?"

The girls glanced at one another uneasily and took chairs across the desk from the stern-faced dean.

Miss Duncan waited. She selected a pencil from her desk and turned it in her fingers, examining it intently.

"I want you girls to know," she said at last, looking up at them, "that your attempts to make friends with Sylvia Reynolds and make her feel at home here in Wellington have been noticed and greatly appreciated. She has a brilliant mind. If she can be persuaded to remain with us, she can become a real credit to Wellington. And I'm sure we can be of help to her."

Felicia straightened. "You–you mean that Sylvia's planning to leave school?"

Miss Duncan nodded. "Precisely. I'm not aware of what is wrong, but she had a phone call from her father this afternoon. Then she told me that she would have to leave at once and ran to her room."

"Oh, that's too bad!" Felicia exclaimed. "And she has been doing so well too!"

"I stopped in to see her this evening," Joan said, "and she had been crying so hard that she could scarcely see."

Miss Duncan's face grew as gentle as they had ever seen it.

"I went up to see her just now, and she said that she couldn't talk to me."

"It must be something terribly serious."

"I'm sure that it is." Miss Duncan turned the pencil slowly in her fingers. "Would you girls do something for me?" she asked. "And for Sylvia?"

"Of course," they echoed.

"Please go up and talk with her," she said. "Try to make her see that she is needed here at Wellington. That we want to help her if we can."

"And if she won't listen to us?" Joan asked. "What do you want us to do then?"

Miss Duncan was silent for a full minute.

"I don't want the poor child to go home alone when she's so upset. Would you take her home and stay with her a few days? That is, if you can't convince her she should remain."

CHAPTER 2

AN UNEXPECTED TRIP

Joan Bailey and Felicia Cartright went out of the office and slowly up the stairs.

"What will we say to her?" Joan asked. "What will we do?"

They stopped in the corridor.

"Let's go into our room and pray first," Felicia said, almost in a whisper. "Then we'll go talk with her."

She led the way into their room, and they knelt together, as they often did now that Joan had made a stand for Christ. Minutes later they went to Sylvia's room and knocked on the door.

There was no answer.

"It's Joan and me, Sylvia," Felicia said again. "We'd like to talk with you."

There was a short silence. Then they heard the bed creak. A moment later the door opened.

"I'm a mess," she said apologetically, brushing her

hair from her eyes with a nervous gesture. "I wasn't going to let anyone come in."

"We'd like to talk with you."

They entered the room, and Sylvia closed the door behind them.

"I'll have to go ahead with my packing," she said. "I'm taking the 1:00 A.M. bus."

Her throat constricted, and for a time she looked away. She swallowed hard and, slamming a sweater into the bag she was packing, tried to close it.

"Here," Joan said, "let me help you."

Sylvia was as quiet and beautiful as her name, a slight, brown-haired girl with blue eyes that smiled even when her lips were too self-conscious to do so. Now the lights had gone out in them, and they were swollen and bloodshot. Her hair, usually so carefully groomed, was disheveled and stringy.

"Do you have to go?" Felicia asked her gently. "We're going to miss you very much."

Sylvia nodded, biting her lower lip.

"Miss Duncan wanted us to come and ask you to stay. She says that you are a real asset to Wellington."

"And that, coming from Miss Duncan, is something," Joan added. "Believe me."

The girl sat down on the bed, clasping and unclasping her hands. She was struggling desperately to control herself.

"Miss Duncan, and all of you, have been very kind. I wish I could stay. You–you'll never know how much

I wish I could stay. These months at Wellington have been the happiest of my life."

"And you're just getting into the swing of things too," Joan went on breezily. "If you think you've had fun this year, wait until next year and the year after. That is when you will really begin to enjoy yourself."

Sylvia Reynolds glanced at them wistfully.

"I've been looking forward to it." She sighed deeply. "But I guess that's all over now."

Felicia put her arm around her tenderly. "Is there anything we can do to help?"

"You have helped already. More than you'll ever know."

It was a long while before she could speak again. "I'll never forget what you two have meant to me."

"Then you really *must* leave Wellington?" Joan asked.

Sylvia bit her lower lip to keep it from trembling and nodded slightly.

"I have to hurry," she said, turning almost brusquely back to her packing. "There's so much to do before the bus leaves."

"Have you eaten?" That was Joan. Calm. Practical.

"I'm not hungry."

"I'll go down to the dining room and bring something up to you. Unless you feel like going down with us to eat."

"Oh, no!" Sylvia answered quickly. "I could not do

that. All I want to do now is get my things together and leave."

She went to the closet and began to pile her clothes on the bed.

Joan started for the door. "I'll go down and get something to eat," she said.

When she was gone, Felicia picked up a beautiful new fur piece and began to examine it.

"Where did you get this, Sylvia? I don't think I ever saw it before."

The other girl turned, picked up the fur, and sat down on the bed.

"Dad made it for me," she said, caressing it gently with her hands. "And sent it to me for my birthday. I–I've been saving it for the formal party next month."

"It's the most beautiful fur piece I've ever seen," Felicia told her. "What is it, silver fox?"

"It's a silver-cross," Sylvia explained. "They're even rarer than a silver fox. If you look closely, you can see the hairs of both the red fox and the silver."

"And it's so soft." She crumpled the hide in her hand. "Why, it's like velvet."

"That's because Dad tanned it for me himself. He learned that from the Native Americans at home." She was working her fingers, lovingly, through the soft fur. "He caught this silver-cross on his trapline. He's a trapper, you know."

"I've often wondered what he did," Felicia answered.

"He used to work in an office in Portland. But after

Mom died, the doctors told him he had to get into something where he could be outdoors. Something about his lungs. So he went back to the thing he knew best."

"It sounds fascinating," Felicia exclaimed, "especially when it means beautiful things like this."

"He could have gotten a good price for this fur, Felicia," the other girl continued, "but he kept it instead and made it up for me. He's always doing things like that." Her throat constricted slightly, and she swallowed hard. "And now he's in some kind of trouble. Serious trouble. And I don't know what it is."

"Then how do you know it's so serious? How can you be sure?"

"It has to be. He was so happy and so proud when I won the scholarship. He said that nothing would have made Mom happier than to know I was going to get a good education. Then today he called and insisted that I come home at once. I just know there's some sort of trouble."

Joan came bustling into the room just then with a tray loaded with milk and sandwiches.

"With an assist from that darling, lovable witch, Miss Duncan, I talked the cook into fixing us something special. Here, come and get something to eat. I had to tell them you were practically starving."

Sylvia smiled wanly. "I am hungry, at that."

"And so am I," Felicia added.

"Me too." Joan opened a milk carton and poured its contents into a glass.

Felicia asked the blessing, praying that God would be with Sylvia Reynolds and her father, and that she would come back to school.

"A lot of good prayer will do," Sylvia exclaimed, almost bitterly. "When Mom was sick, Dad and I prayed and prayed and prayed. But it didn't do any good." Her voice trembled on the brink of tears.

Joan and Felicia looked at her tenderly. "We're sorry for you, Sylvia. Truly we are."

When they finished eating, Joan Bailey turned to her roommate.

"I take it that we're going to Maine."

Sylvia looked at her quizzically. "What do you mean?"

"Miss Duncan suddenly had a twinge of conscience over the way she has been working me," the dark-haired girl said breezily. "So when she learned that you were leaving, she called us into her office and said, "Joan, you've been studying much too hard lately.'"

"That *is* a joke," Felicia broke in.

"My dear," Joan retorted, lifting her eyebrows, "you are ruining my story. Completely ruining my story. Now I'll have to start all over."

"Oh, no! Not that."

Even Sylvia laughed a little.

"What Joan is trying to say," Felicia continued,

"is that Miss Duncan thought it would be nice for us to drive you home and stay with you a few days."

"But–but everybody has already done so much for me," the girl protested.

"That is, if you'd like to have us," Felicia added.

"If I'd like to have you!" she exclaimed. "It would be wonderful. I've been dreading that long ride alone on the bus.

They started at dawn the following morning in Joan's car. Driving was slow over the icy, winding roads, and it was almost dark before they reached the little northern Maine cabin where Sylvia and her father lived.

"It's not much of a place," she said apologetically before they reached it. "Just a five-room cabin on Snider's Pond, but it's so quiet and beautiful here that I wouldn't trade it for any other spot on earth."

Joan had slowed the car to a crawl when they left the main road and followed the single lane of the snowplow. The girls looked about appreciatively – at the great, smooth-barked beech trees so straight and tall above the evergreens; at the snow piled high on stone fences and posts; at the snowbirds that flitted busily along the road.

"It is beautiful," Felicia said, her voice low, as though fearful of breaking the enchanted spell that had been woven around them. "It is beautiful, Sylvia."

Harold Reynolds came out to greet them. He was

a tall, graying man with shoulders that were stooped and a face that was lined with care.

"Oh, Dad!" Sylvia cried, running to him. "I've been so worried since I got your phone call. Are you all right?"

His silence was startling. He took Sylvia in his arms and held her momentarily. Then he released her and smiled at Joan and Felicia.

"I thought you would be coming by bus."

"That's what I planned," she said, "but Miss Duncan and the girls insisted that they bring me home."

She introduced them to him. He acknowledged the introduction gravely and noted the skis on the top carrier.

"I see you're planning on a little vacation going back."

"We just didn't take them off after last Saturday," Joan said, smiling. "It looks as though there's some good skiing here."

His face grew grim. "I'm afraid that we have very little to offer the ski fan," he said, his voice growing cold. "There is skiing, of course, but most of it is a matter of necessity."

Felicia and Joan glanced at one another.

His face softened in a moment or two.

"We're so grateful to you," he said, "for coming all this way to bring Sylvia home. I wish it were possible for you to spend the night with us."

"Oh, but they're going to, Dad," Sylvia broke in

quickly. "We've driven all day, and I know they must be exhausted. Besides I–I won't want them to leave."

If he was disturbed, he gave no sign. "Oh, they're welcome enough!" he said, smiling. "You know that your friends are always welcome. But our place isn't very fancy. I thought perhaps they wouldn't care to stay with us."

They lingered at the dinner table that evening, talking with forced cheerfulness. Mr. Reynolds spoke very little. His dark, weather-lined face was somber. And every now and then, he looked past the little group at the table as though his thoughts were far away. Every now and then, he tugged at his ear or scratched the side of his nose with his thumbnail nervously. It was he who suggested that they turn in.

"I'm terribly tired," he said, "and I know that you girls have had a hard day too."

"And did you notice, Felicia," Joan asked softly when the two of them were alone together in their room, "how he tried to discourage us about skiing and even staying with them for the night?"

Felicia nodded. "He seemed anxious to be rid of us," she said. "And I don't think it's because he's unfriendly. He seems to be a very nice person, and he treats us like queens."

Joan crossed to the frost-etched window and looked out into the brilliant moonlit night. "But Sylvia is right," she said. "Mr. Reynolds is in some serious trouble. Did you notice how he avoided her question when she asked him what was wrong?"

"And that look in his eyes when he thought no one was watching." She shuddered. "There's something terribly wrong here."

Joan got her Bible and opened it to the place where they had been reading for devotions.

The following morning before daylight the girls heard someone bustling about in the kitchen.

"I think we'd better get up," Felicia Cartright said. "Somebody is fixing breakfast."

"Breakfast?" Joan echoed, turning over and squinting at her watch sleepily. "Who'd want breakfast at this hour? It's practically the middle of the night."

"Don't be so lazy," her friend countered, getting up and pulling off her covers. "It's six o'clock. It'll do you good to get up early for once."

Reluctantly Joan crawled out of bed and dressed.

When they went into the other room, they were surprised to see that it wasn't Sylvia at all. Mr. Reynolds was standing at the stove frying bacon. He had already set the table and had the coffee pot perking merrily.

"Thought I'd get up and get breakfast for you," he explained. "So you can get an early start back to Wellington."

Sylvia, who had just come out of her bedroom in her robe and slippers, looked at the girls with something akin to desperation.

"You don't have to leave today, do you?" she asked.

"Now Sylvia," her father said. "It has been very kind of the girls to come all this way to bring you home. We can't impose on them any more than we have already."

"But I'm sure that it would be all right with Miss Duncan. You will stay, won't you? Please!"

CHAPTER 3

WILD RUMORS

Felicia Cartright looked at Sylvia understandingly. "We'll talk it over," she promised. "And if we feel that we can spare a few days, we'll stay."

"That's very kind of you," Harold Reynolds said, "but, Sylvia, don't you think we have imposed upon the girls enough? After all, they have their studies, and they've made a sacrifice in time to come up here."

"But Dad," she repeated, her voice quavering, "I want them to stay."

"It's all right with me," he said reluctantly. "I just don't want to get the girls into trouble at school. That's all."

"You won't have to worry about that," Joan answered. "Miss Duncan had a weak moment and told us to take off as much time as necessary."

They had breakfast together around the kitchen table, and the girls helped Sylvia with the dishes.

Mr. Reynolds got into his heavy coat and picked up his snowshoes.

"I'll probably be back about noon," he told his daughter. "I want to say goodbye to you two," he said, shaking hands with Felicia and Joan, "in case you should decide to leave this morning."

"But they are going to stay," Sylvia said quickly. "For three or four days anyway."

"We'll see," Felicia told him.

Darkness was just beginning to retreat from the somber gray cast of dawn as Harold Reynolds went slogging off through the deep snow.

Sylvia stood at the door watching until he was out of sight.

"Don't pay any attention to what Dad said just now," she told them. "He's so upset that he doesn't realize what he's saying."

"We really should be getting back," Felicia said. "We'll have our work to make up, and that's never easy."

"You can say that again," Joan added. "I know. I'm the champion 'maker-upper' at Wellington."

Sylvia sat down at the kitchen table wearily, as though her strength had ebbed away leaving her exhausted.

"When you girls first came to my room the other night, I wanted you to go away," she said listlessly. "All I cared about was being alone. But I can't bear the thought of being alone now. At least not right away."

"But what can we do?" Joan asked.

She shook her head.

"I don't know what anyone can do," she replied, "but I feel as if I–I'll go all to pieces if you leave me now."

Joan and Felicia looked at one another briefly.

"What do you say, Joan?"

"Why don't we wait until tomorrow at least? Besides, I'd like to unlimber those skis of mine. You do have some good hills for it, don't you?"

Sylvia brightened noticeably. "As soon as we get these dishes done, I'll show you the finest hill for skiing that you ever saw. It's as good as the best places in the White Mountains, only without all the people."

"Now that sounds wonderful to me."

They skied the morning away on the steep hill Sylvia took them to. When they came back for lunch, they were weary.

"I'm exhausted," Joan said, sprawling into a chair. "Let's warm up some soup and take a nap."

"You girls go ahead and lie down," Sylvia said when they had finished eating. "I'll wait for Dad. He ought to be along any time now."

"You aren't going to have to suggest that again," Felicia said. "I think I could sleep all afternoon."

They went into their room and were just dozing off when Harold Reynolds came back to the cabin, stamping the snow off his boots.

"The girls' car is still here, I suppose they decided to stay."

"Until tomorrow anyway."

There was a short pause. "Where are they now?" He lowered his voice, but they could still hear him plainly.

"We went skiing this morning. They wanted to take a nap. They must be asleep by this time."

"You shouldn't have asked them to stay, Sylvia." His voice grew harsh.

"But, Dad," she protested, "they're the best friends I had at Wellington. I just couldn't bear to think of having them leave."

"You shouldn't have done it, Sylvia," he repeated. "The main reason I wanted to get you out of Wellington was so this story wouldn't get back to the school." He was breathing heavily. "I can't run the risk of having you embarrassed in front of your friends."

"Whatever are you talking about? Nothing you have ever done would embarrass me." She spoke confidently.

"The gossip that's going around Morrisville would embarrass you," he said bitterly. "And if your friends stay very long, they're going to hear it. It isn't myself that I'm thinking of. It's you."

"What is it, Dad?" she asked seriously. "What's wrong?"

He was silent for a time. And when he spoke his

voice was numb and lifeless. "All I can tell you now, Sylvia," he said, "is that there's not a bit of truth in it."

"If you'd only tell me, Dad," she said, her voice taut, "maybe we could help prove that you aren't guilty."

"I've lived in these parts since before your mother and I were married," he went on. "During that time I can't remember lying to anyone or taking a penny that wasn't rightfully mine." He sighed deeply. "But people won't remember those things. They'd rather believe a string of silly rumors. There isn't anything that anyone can do."

"I can't have you feeling that way," she told him.

"Now, Sylvia, don't worry about this. It'll all work out." He laughed shortly. "And if you want the girls to stay, it's all right with me. Only we can't let them find out what people are saying."

Joan and Felicia looked at one another, pity in their eyes.

"Did you hear that?" Felicia whispered. "We've got to help them, Joan. Even if it's only to stand by and let them know we believe in them regardless of what people are saying."

The girls lay in bed for an hour or more, staring up at the ceiling. Sleep was far away.

At last they got up and went back into the kitchen, carrying their shoes.

"So you finally decided to get up," Sylvia said with forced cheerfulness. "You're just in time to go along to the store. Dad tells me that we're about out of groceries."

Morrisville was a small county seat town with the imprint of the woods heavily on it. The stores carried traps and heavy caliber rifles beside wide displays of double-bitted axes and power saws. The walks had been shoveled that morning, and the snow was piled high along the curb.

"We'll stop here at the grocery store," Sylvia said. "You can come in with me if you like. There'll probably be plenty of boxes for us to carry out from the looks of this list Dad gave me."

Half a dozen men were seated at the back of the store, talking leisurely. Sylvia spoke to all of them. They smiled warmly. It was easy to see what they thought of her.

"I didn't know you were back, Miss Sylvia," the clerk said as he put her groceries in boxes.

"I'm going to be home for a while," she said without explanation.

He glanced at her. "You tell that dad of yours that we're all plugging for him," he said softly as he gave her the change.

She flushed scarlet.

"Here," Felicia said. "Let us help you with those groceries."

She and Joan each took a large box and started for the door. As they left the building, a burly trapper came swaggering up to Sylvia.

"Good afternoon, Sylvia," he said, his words thickly accented. He was a short man and dark. His face was brown and weather beaten, and his hair bushed out from under his cap at the ears and the back of his neck.

"Hello, Pierre!" she replied.

Felicia noted the sharpness in her voice.

"I hear you come back from that fancy school," Pierre Dufeld went on. "It is because they have finally caught up to that thieving father of yours. No?"

For a long, heart-breaking moment, time ceased. The color fled from her face and neck, and her whole being trembled.

"My dad is not a thief," she retorted, her temper rising. "And you ought to know it better than most. You've lived and trapped next to him long enough."

The French-Canadian's face was twisted evilly. "Tell me, Sylvia, when do they put him in jail?"

"Come on," Joan said firmly. "Let's get out of here."

"When do they put him in jail?"

Sylvia put the groceries in the back seat of the car without answering him.

"When they lock him up like he deserves," Pierre called after her, "you not be so smart."

Sylvia sat very quiet in the car while Joan drove home. "Well," she said at last, "now you know."

"And we don't believe a word of it," Joan affirmed. "The things that a man like that says don't mean anything."

"The people in and around Morrisville who really count know your father well enough to have confidence in him. They're not going to believe any wild rumors," Felicia added.

"Do you really think they won't?" Sylvia asked, brightening.

"Of course not."

It was Felicia who saw a car pull up to the cabin door. "Why, look," she said, "we've got company."

"Oh!" Sylvia exclaimed.

The other girls stared at her. "What's wrong?" Joan asked.

"That's Sheriff Anderson's car." Her voice was suddenly lifeless. "What do you suppose he's doing here?"

The sheriff, who had been sitting behind the wheel, got out and came over to them.

"Good afternoon, Sylvia," he said uneasily. "I've been waiting to talk with your dad, but he doesn't seem to be around."

"He was here when we left."

The sheriff glanced at his watch. "I'm going to have to leave in a few minutes. Do you suppose you could spare me a few minutes?"

"Sure," she answered. "Won't you come in?" And then she remembered Felicia and Joan. "You can talk in front of my friends. They–they want to help us."

The sheriff was obviously disturbed. He followed the girls into the cabin and took a seat near the fire.

"This won't take more than a minute or two," he

said. "Did you ever see this?" He took a small, green medallion from his pocket and handed it to her.

She looked at it intently.

"Why, yes," she said at last. "That's the medallion my mother won in a spelling contest years ago when she was in school. Dad has carried it for years and years."

Sheriff Anderson's face grew tense and grim. He took a deep breath.

"That," he said, "is exactly what I've been afraid of."

CHAPTER 4

THE SHERIFF'S VISIT

Sylvia Reynolds' mouth went dry, and beads of perspiration dotted her forehead. She massaged her throat nervously.

"What is this all about, Sheriff Anderson?" she asked. "And what does this green medallion of Mom's have to do with it?"

"I'm not exactly sure, Sylvia." He spoke reluctantly, forcing the words out one by one. "That is why I wanted to talk with your dad. The chances are there is a simple, logical explanation."

She moistened her lips with the tip of her tongue.

"I guess you know how hard this is for me. I've known your father for more than twenty years. We've been good friends. Very good friends."

She went over and built up the fire again. He waited until she had finished.

"I've been told that you have a beautiful new

silver-cross fur piece, Sylvia," he went on at last. "Is that correct?"

"Dad gave it to me for my birthday. Would you like to see it?"

"If you don't mind."

He took it from her when she brought it and examined it carefully. "It certainly fits the description. I may have to take it in later, Sylvia, or bring someone out to identify it."

"Dad caught this fur himself," she said confidently.

"I hope that's right," he told her. "For your sake and your dad's, I hope that's right."

She stared at him quizzically. "Sheriff Anderson," she began, "everyone is making remarks to me, but no one will tell me anything. Please, just what is going on? What does everyone think Dad has done?"

"I wouldn't say that everyone thinks he has done anything," he said, moving back a little from the stove. "As a matter of fact, he has a lot of friends in and around Morrisville. But there are a few stories out." He paused and thoughtfully examined the green medallion in his hand.

"I know all that," she said. "But what are those stories? No one will tell me."

He sighed. "I guess I owe you an explanation. Besides you'll find out soon enough. There has been an outbreak of fur stealing this winter," he said. "Most everyone has had trouble, except your dad. That has caused the other trappers to ask questions."

"Dad wouldn't steal any furs!" she said, straightening defiantly. "He wouldn't steal anything."

"I checked with the fur buyers. Your dad sold more pelts so far this year than he did all of last year."

"He's had a run of good luck," Sylvia countered. "That isn't against the law."

"No," the officer went on softly, "but we also checked the inventory of the furs that were stolen. He sold more of every species than was reported stolen. As far as the figures are concerned, he could have stolen them and still sold those he trapped himself."

"But that's not evidence," she protested. "Not real evidence."

"I realize that, and your dad hasn't been arrested yet either. That's enough to tell you that our evidence is not conclusive. However, there are other things that point in Harold's direction."

"Such as–"

"That silver-cross fur piece for one thing," he said. "It fits the general description we were given. The fact that your dad has been hard pressed to keep you in school is another."

"I've been at Wellington on a scholarship."

"It has meant a financial burden for him. He told me so himself. That would provide the motive. And a big one." He took the green medallion from his pocket and tossed it into the air. "And take this medallion for another thing. It was found on the floor of the last place where furs were reported stolen!"

"Oh, no!" Sylvia cried out in protest.

"So you see, Sylvia," the officer went on slowly, "while it's been mostly gossip and rumor up until this point, evidence is beginning to show up that is strong enough to start giving it attention."

"I–I don't know what to say. Could–could it be that there is another medallion like Mom's? Or almost like it?"

"That's entirely possible. That is one of the things I wanted to talk with Harold about." He looked at his watch again. "I'm sorry that I have to be going. I'd like to talk with him tonight. But I have an appointment in town in an hour. You tell him I was out, won't you?"

She nodded mechanically.

When the sheriff was gone, she stood at the door for a long while staring after him. Joan and Felicia came up and put their arms around her.

"I know he didn't do it," she said, her voice numb with fear. "I don't care what the evidence is or what they say. I know he didn't do it."

"Of course, he didn't," Joan replied. "There's a logical explanation for all of this. The thing we've got to do is find it."

"And we will too," Felicia added confidently, "with God's help."

They were still standing there when the Cartright girl heard something at the window. Heard it or felt it, she wasn't sure which. An uneasy feeling began to creep over her. She turned and glanced nervously in that direction.

"What's the matter, Felicia?" Joan asked.

"Do you hear anything?"

"I hear you."

"Anything else, stupid?"

They were silent for a moment, listening breathlessly. Then Felicia inched toward the door.

"There's someone out there," she whispered.

"Are you sure?" Sylvia asked.

She nodded slightly. "Are you game to go with me and find out?"

"You don't mean that you're going out there and–and ask for trouble?" Joan demanded.

"You can wait here if you want to, but Sylvia and I are going out there."

Felicia jerked open the door and dashed outside. Joan and Sylvia followed her. "Around this way," the Cartright girl gasped.

They ran around the cabin in the deep snow.

"See!" Joan exclaimed. "There's no one here, and I'm not going to be very long. It's cold!"

"There's no one here now," Sylvia said excitedly. "But look, someone has been here. There are the marks of his snowshoes."

The girls stared intently at the deep tracks in the snow.

"W-w-what do you suppose he was doing?"

"Maybe the sheriff made those tracks while he

was waiting for your dad," Joan Bailey said skeptically. "He could have gone around to the window to make sure no one was home."

"He didn't have snowshoes," Sylvia countered. "And besides, those tracks lead over that way. From the looks of them the man must have been in a terrible hurry."

"He probably scooted out when Felicia said that she heard him." Joan turned back toward the cabin, her teeth chattering. "Let's get our coats and skis," she suggested, hurrying inside, "and follow those tracks to see where that guy went. It might help prove Mr. Reynolds' innocence to know who that guy is and what he was doing at our window."

"Maybe it would be better to follow those tracks tomorrow," Felicia suggested. "Then we'll know that whoever made them isn't lying out there in the brush waiting to grab us."

"That's a good idea at that," Joan said, "even if you did come up with it."

It wasn't long until Harold Reynolds returned. As soon as Sylvia heard him stamping the snow off his boots, she ran and unlatched the door.

"Wow, it's getting cold outside," he told them with affected cheerfulness. "Almost makes a guy wish he lived in Texas or Louisiana."

"Dad," Sylvia said, her voice small and thin, "you had company this afternoon. Sheriff Anderson was here to see you."

He looked up with surprise.

"I've been expecting him." He went over to the stove, shook down the ashes, and put in two or three pieces of wood. "Did he say what he wanted?"

"I–I," she swallowed hard, "I guess he wanted to talk with you."

There was a short silence.

"I suppose he'll be out again tomorrow," Harold said lamely, "if it's important."

Sylvia Reynolds was breathing heavily.

"Dad," she managed at last, "have you still got that green medallion you used to carry? The one Mom won in the spelling contest?"

A strange, blank look crossed his face. For a moment he did not speak.

"Do you still have it?" she asked desperately.

Slowly he shook his head.

"I wasn't going to tell you, Sylvia. I know it meant so much to you. I've kept thinking that I'd run across it. But I haven't. In fact, it's been a month or so since I remember seeing it. I must have mislaid it somewhere."

Sylvia Reynolds looked at her friends. Desperation and anguish wrote their messages in their eyes.

CHAPTER 5

TRACKS IN THE SNOW

Felicia Cartright and Joan Bailey excused themselves and went to bed.

"I feel very sorry for Sylvia," Joan said in a whisper when they were in bed. "Imagine how terrible it would be to have people think that your father was a thief."

Her companion nodded.

"And the worst of it is that there seems to be such a mountain of evidence. That green medallion was actually found at the place where some of the furs were stolen. And now the authorities have traced it to Mr. Reynolds. Poor Sylvia! I just can't imagine how she must feel."

Joan was silent for a long while.

"Do you suppose he's really guilty?" she asked at last.

"I don't see how he can be," Felicia answered. "He

seems so honest and genuine." She sighed deeply. "But wouldn't it be terrible if he were?"

The following morning Mr. Reynolds had already gone out into the woods when Joan and Felicia got up. Sylvia was sitting in the kitchen alone, staring at the stove.

"Are you up already?" Joan asked, trying to be cheerful.

"I had breakfast with Dad this morning."

"I thought Joan never was going to waken," Felicia said, "and I was just about as bad." She saw Sylvia's blood-shot eyes. "How did you sleep?" she asked.

"As a matter of fact, I didn't sleep at all." Sylvia spoke listlessly, as though she cared little anymore. "I don't think I even closed my eyes all night. All I could see was that medallion. All I could hear was Dad saying that he didn't have it and the sheriff saying that it had been found at Myron Baker's, where the last furs were stolen."

"I'll admit that it looks bad," Felicia said, "but we can't dwell on that. We've got to get busy and ferret out the truth. We've got to prove that your dad is innocent."

"But don't you realize what this does?" Sylvia asked, her voice rising. "It practically proves that Dad is guilty. A jury would never believe that he was telling the truth against evidence like that." Her lower lip started to tremble. "I don't know what I'd do if they would arrest him. And that's what's going to happen, in spite of everything."

Felicia Cartright pulled up a chair and sat down beside her. "You know, Sylvia," she said tenderly, "you don't have to carry this load alone. Why don't you put your trust in Jesus and ask Him to give you the strength to help you through this?"

Sylvia did not answer.

"Jesus said to come to Him, you who are weary and burdened, and He will give you rest," Felicia said. "He will help you."

"Nothing can help now," Sylvia countered numbly. "Nothing can help."

Felicia got to her feet and busied herself with the stove.

"I know one thing we've got to do today," Joan said after several minutes. "And that is to follow those snowshoe tracks and see where they go."

"That's right." Felicia began to set the table, and Sylvia came over to help her. "Maybe we'll get a lead that way."

"Then I think we ought to go over to the Bakers' house," Sylvia suggested. "There's just a chance – an outside chance – that we can dig up some information there."

They had breakfast and went out into the chilly morning air to follow the tracks of the person who had stood beneath the cabin window the night before.

"He was in a hurry," Sylvia said, pointing to the

long, sliding imprints of the snowshoes. "A big hurry. We must have frightened him."

"Then that makes us even," Joan put in. "He certainly frightened us."

They fastened on their skis and followed the trail in the soft snow. The guy had indeed been in a hurry. He had gone stumbling and sliding over drifts, through trees and around clumps of brush, until he reached the main road. There he had taken off his snowshoes and gotten into a car.

"What do you know!" Joan exclaimed.

The girls examined the tracks and looked at one another in amazement.

"Now why would anyone drive over here in a car and sneak up to look in your cabin, Sylvia?" Felicia asked.

The other girl shook her head. "It would have to be something important for him to go to all that trouble."

"And secretive," the Cartright girl added. "He walked more than a mile on snowshoes through the forest when he could have driven directly to the cabin."

"The fact that he ran means that he didn't want to be seen," Joan added.

Felicia's face lit up. "We have our first clue!"

"But what does it mean?"

She thought for a moment. "It means that someone is interested or concerned about what's going on at your cabin, Sylvia. They're interested enough to go to all that trouble just to find out."

Joan was examining the snowshoe tracks carefully.

"I thought perhaps we could find something distinctive about these," she said, "but I don't believe so."

"They're just an ordinary pair of commercial snowshoes," Sylvia announced. "Half the people up here use the same kind."

"Then there's nothing there," Felicia murmured. "What about the car tracks? They say that something can be learned from them."

"If you know how to read them," Joan replied. "Frankly, they all look alike to me."

"I guess it doesn't matter. A truck or something has been along here and spoiled them."

"But we do know that someone else besides the sheriff and us is interested in what's going on. That's a great deal."

They debated their next course of action and finally decided to go to the Baker cabin to look at the room where the medallion had been found.

"I don't know what we can find over there," the Cartright girl said, "but it's a starting place."

"And," Joan cautioned, "I don't think we ought to say anything about the guy at the window to anyone just yet."

"Should we drive over to the Bakers' house?" Sylvia asked as they returned to the cabin.

"When we can ski?" Joan echoed.

"It'll take us a little longer," Sylvia replied impatiently. "That was the only thing I was thinking."

"It might be better to ski at that," Felicia said. "It will give us a chance to see if there are any more strange snowshoe tracks around."

They skied back to the cabin, ate lunch, left a note for Mr. Reynolds, and set off across the hills for the Baker place.

"We cross Dad's trapline," Sylvia said. "What should we tell him if we see him? About where we're going, I mean."

"The truth if he asks us," Felicia advised. "Nothing if he doesn't."

They had traveled almost a mile when the Reynolds girl stopped suddenly. "Look down there," she said, pointing at a dark figure on the other side of the creek.

"That isn't your dad, is it?"

Sylvia shook her head. "Dad's much taller than that, but that is his trapline."

The guy turned their way, stared momentarily, and then went plunging into the brush.

"Maybe we can follow him," Joan suggested impulsively. "He's probably the guy who was snooping around the cabin last night. If he's stealing from your dad's traps, the chances are that he's the one who stole the rest of the furs."

But Sylvia shook her head.

"Dad hasn't had any traps robbed or pelts stolen

all winter," she protested. "Why would anyone start now?"

"We don't have to follow him," Felicia said, "but I think we ought to go down that way and see if any of your dad's traps are disturbed, Sylvia."

Slowly, hesitantly, they made their way down the bank and across the creek.

"Now whatever you do," Joan said apprehensively, "keep your eyes open, and if you see anything that looks as though it's coming our way, run!"

Felicia laughed nervously. "How do you run uphill on skis?"

"Never you mind how you run uphill on skis," her friend retorted. "If that guy comes charging out of the brush, you just watch me, and you'll see how it's done."

They hadn't intended to follow the man's trail, but when they came across it, they followed it for three or four hundred yards. He had made his way along the bank, stopping every now and then to go down to the stream.

"This is the place where he must have first seen us," Sylvia said. "He didn't even lift his snowshoes as he shuffled behind the brush."

"And look!" Joan added. "See how deep these tracks are! He must have stood here for some time watching us. Then he went up the hill." She paused, shivering. "Do you suppose he's in the woods some-where watching us?"

"You can think of the most pleasant things!" Felicia told her.

"Do you suppose he's the same guy who was outside the cabin window last night?" Joan asked after a moment or two.

"There's no way of knowing," the Cartright girl said. "Didn't you say that most of the people used the same kind of snowshoes, Sylvia?"

She nodded. "But whoever this guy was, we know that he's up to something or he wouldn't have hidden this way. When he saw us coming, he would have stopped and talked with us."

"Maybe he's stealing from your dad's traps," Joan said again.

"But we've passed three or four of them," Sylvia said, "and he didn't even lift them to see whether Dad had anything or not." She paused momentarily. "No, I think he must be after something else."

"But what else could he be after?" Felicia asked.

"Dad is a good trapper. One of the best. And a number of the others are jealous of him. It could be that someone is trying to take his trapline away from him. That could account for what's been going on."

"You mean that someone might be framing this whole thing just in order to get his trapline?" Felicia wanted to know.

"It could be that," Sylvia said thoughtfully, "or it could be that someone thinks Dad is going to be arrested right away and wants to grab off the trapline before someone else gets it."

They stood there for several minutes talking when Joan looked up at the sun. It was already slipping behind the trees.

"Do you know that it's going to be dark in a little while?" she asked. "How far is it over to the Bakers' place?"

Sylvia glanced up. "Oh," she exclaimed, "I had no idea it was so late! We've still got a mile and a half to their place, and it will be dark in half an hour."

"With everything that's been happening around here," Joan said, "I'd just as soon wait until the cold, hard light of day to go traipsing around these woods."

"Besides," Felicia added, "I don't think we'd have time enough to look around the way we want to."

They turned and went back to the Reynolds' cabin. When they got there, Sylvia's dad was already home. Smoke was pouring invitingly from the chimney.

"Well," he said, with forced cheer, "have you girls had enough skiing for one day?"

"Right now, all we're interested in is a fire and an easy chair," Joan said, standing her skis up beside the cabin door.

"I'm disappointed," he told her. "I thought I'd be able to interest you in some venison steak."

"You needn't be disappointed, Mr. Reynolds," Felicia said, laughing. "I've seen Joan awfully tired, but I never did see her too tired to eat."

"My friend!"

They sat down at the table, Joan asked the blessing, and Mr. Reynolds passed them a big platter of steak.

"This is the last of the deer I killed during the season," he said. "When I was in town this afternoon, I went into the locker and got it. Thought you would like to try some venison."

"It's delicious."

"Dad," Sylvia said, when the meal was almost over, "have you noticed anyone down along your trapline lately?"

"I haven't seen anyone," he replied, "but to tell you the truth, I've seen a lot of evidence that someone has been along there. Nothing missing, though." He looked at her curiously. "Why?"

"We were skiing down that way," she explained, "and saw a guy. He hid in the brush and then took off when we headed in that direction."

Mr. Reynolds held out his cup, and she filled it with coffee. "Someone who can't wait to take over my trapline, I suppose."

For two or three minutes, the girls listened to music playing on Mr. Reynold's radio.

"By the way, Sylvia," Mr. Reynolds said suddenly, "I was looking in that old jacket of mine on the porch a little while ago, and I found this." He tossed a small round object to her.

"The green medallion!" she exclaimed. "Oh, Dad! I'm so glad we found it."

"So am I. I've carried it for years. I can't figure out how it came to be in that jacket. I always carry it in a trouser pocket."

"You've got it back," she said thankfully. "That's the important thing."

Joan and Felicia looked at one another and smiled.

The music on the radio stopped, and the crisp, firm voice of the announcer came on.

"And now for the news," he said. "The sheriff's office was broken into late last night or early this morning, Sheriff Anderson announced a few minutes ago. Nothing of value was taken except a piece of evidence the sheriff has been holding in the fur theft investigation. He declined to say what it was. . . ."

The color fled from Sylvia Reynolds' face. Her fingers relaxed, almost lifelessly, and her cup clattered resoundingly to the table.

CHAPTER 6

THE STOLEN EVIDENCE

For a brief, agonizing moment no one in the little cabin spoke. Felicia's head spun. Suddenly she was desperately tired. Sylvia's eyes reflected the horror that seized her. Her throat tightened, and she moistened her lips with the tip of her tongue.

"What's the matter with you girls?" Mr. Reynolds asked, staring from one to the other. "You look as though you'd just seen a ghost. I thought you'd be glad to know that I found the medallion."

"Dad," Sylvia said softly when she could speak, "didn't you hear the radio just now?"

"Oh, sure," he said, "but I can't let those things bother me. If I did, I wouldn't be able to think of anything else."

"But Dad!" she protested. "When Sheriff Anderson was out here, he showed us that medallion." Her eyes bored into his. "He said it had been found on the floor on the Bakers' property, in the shed where their furs had been stolen."

Harold Reynolds was incredulous. He took the medallion from his pocket and stared at it. "But that couldn't be," he murmured. "I've got it right here. It couldn't have been found in the Bakers' shed."

The silence was electric.

"It was found over there, Dad," Sylvia repeated. "Sheriff Anderson had it. He told us that it was the most important piece of evidence he had in the fur theft case." She took a deep breath. "Now the sheriff's office has been broken into, and an important piece of evidence has been stolen. And–and, Dad," she continued miserably, "you've got the medallion again!"

Harold Reynolds stiffened. The color ebbed from his cheeks, and perspiration beaded his forehead. His eyes were staring.

"I can't understand it," he muttered. "I can't understand it at all." He turned the medallion thoughtfully, rubbing it between his fingers. He started to speak again, then stopped.

"What are we going to do now, Dad?" Sylvia asked.

He got to his feet and walked slowly over to the window, where he stood staring out into the crisp night air.

"What are we going to do?" Her voice rose hysterically.

He turned to face her. "It's too late to do anything tonight," he said. "But in the morning, we'll have to go and see Sheriff Anderson at once."

"Oh, no!" she cried, her hand flying to her lips. "If he finds out that you've got the medallion, he'll be sure that you stole it. That you took the furs and everything." Her voice choked off in desperation.

Her dad came over and took her by the shoulders tenderly. "It doesn't matter what he thinks, Sylvia," he said. "It matters, of course, but it can't affect what we do or don't do. He has been holding this medallion as evidence. I'll have to take it back to him."

Sylvia turned to her companions.

"Won't you help me reason with him?" she asked. "The sheriff will arrest Dad if he goes in and hands him this medallion. He'll be positive, then, that Dad stole the furs and the medallion because it was evidence. He'll be thrown into jail and–and–I'd just die if that happens."

"Your father is right, Sylvia," Felicia told her as gently as possible. "The green medallion is a piece of evidence. An important piece of evidence. As your dad says, he has no right to keep it, regardless of how incriminating it might be."

She turned to Joan, helplessly, for support.

"I've got to agree with them," the Bailey girl said. "The truth is hard, but it's the only honorable way. And in the long run, it's the best way, even though it might not seem to be."

Sylvia sighed her resignation. "Well," she said at last, "if you're determined to give the medallion to the sheriff, we're going with you."

He smiled wanly.

"Now, Sylvia," he said, "it's not going to be as bad as all that. We'll go to bed, get a good night's rest, and in the morning, we'll turn the medallion over to Sheriff Anderson. Now don't worry about it."

The girls did the dishes mechanically, making only brief, halfhearted attempts at conversation. Mr. Reynolds stood at the window for a long while, staring out across the little clearing.

"Felicia," Sylvia whispered tensely before they went to bed, "you'll pray for Dad, won't you?" Her quavering voice revealed her desperation.

"Of course. And we'll be praying for you too. Not only that this whole affair works out for you, but that you will accept the Lord Jesus as your Savior."

"I'd do it right now," Sylvia said fervently, "if I were sure that God would help Dad get out of this without having to go to jail. If I just knew that He'd help prove that Dad is innocent."

But Felicia Cartright shook her head.

"We do not come to Jesus that way," she answered. "We must come to Him because we realize that we are sinners and need a Savior. Because we are tired of sin and want to be born again. According to the Bible that's the only way. We can't bargain with God."

Tears welled in Sylvia's eyes. She wanted to speak but could not. Instead, she took hold of Felicia's arm and squeezed it hard.

That night Felicia and Joan spent a long while on their knees, praying for Mr. Reynolds and Sylvia.

"I don't know when I've ever felt so helpless," Joan Bailey whispered when they were in bed. "Just when we thought things were looking up and we were beginning to uncover some evidence that would help prove that Mr. Reynolds wasn't guilty, this had to happen."

Before breakfast the next morning, Sylvia's dad went out and started the car to let it warm up. And as soon as they finished eating, he got into his coat.

"We're going to have to hurry," he said. "Ed gets out early in the morning when he's working on a case. He might be gone if we lose much time."

Sylvia was biting her lower lip as they went out and got into the car.

The sheriff was in his office when they got there.

"I'm glad you came in, Harold," he said. "I was going to drive out to your place this morning as soon as I finished looking over my mail."

"I thought probably you'd be around," Mr. Reynolds said. He handed the officer the medallion and told him where he had found it.

"You realize that this medallion is the strongest bit of evidence against you that we have, Harold," Mr. Anderson said.

"I know that."

"And you say you found this medallion on your back porch yesterday afternoon?"

"That's right. In the pocket of an old jacket. I don't know how long it was there or how it got there, but that's where I found it yesterday."

"You aren't going to put him in jail, are you, Sheriff Anderson?" Sylvia demanded.

Mr. Anderson shook his head.

"No, Sylvia," he said, weighing the medallion in his hand. "I'm not going to put your dad in jail. If I had my way about it, I'd drop the whole investigation right now."

"What do you mean?"

He turned to Mr. Reynolds. "I know that the fact that you brought this medallion back to me isn't the sort of evidence that could be admitted in your defense in court," he said, "but it goes to underline what I've believed about you all along, Harold. Even though there is a certain amount of evidence and talk that points to you, I'm becoming more convinced than ever that you're innocent."

"Thanks, Ed," Mr. Reynolds replied, smiling. "It's good to know that I've got one friend in and around Morrisville."

"Of course," he hastened to add, "what I think personally and what I may have to do as sheriff are two entirely different things."

Sylvia's dad nodded.

Sheriff Anderson followed them to the door. "I think it would be wise," he said, "if you don't say anything to anyone about finding this medallion and returning it to me. Sometimes an investigation is easier to carry on when all the information isn't common knowledge."

CHAPTER 7

THE GIRLS SEARCH FOR CLUES

Y ou have no idea how much better I feel," Sylvia said when they were back at the Reynolds' cabin and were alone together. "It seems as though a terrific burden has been taken off my shoulders."

"I guess we feel the same way," Joan Bailey said. "We just felt sick when the announcer said that an important piece of evidence had been stolen, and your dad had just shown us the medallion."

"And the best part of it is," Sylvia went on, "that Sheriff Anderson thinks Dad is innocent, and he's going to try to find evidence to prove it."

"It's always best to face up to things," Felicia told them, "regardless of how unpleasant it might seem at first. Did you stop to think that the sheriff was on his way out to your place, Sylvia? Since the medallion pointed so directly to your dad, that was naturally the first place he would think of checking. He'd have found it, and the chances are that your dad would be in jail right now."

"I don't like to remind you two of this," Joan said in her matter-of-fact way, "but we can't forget that we still don't have any real evidence that proves your dad is innocent. And there is considerable circumstantial evidence that still points to him. As the sheriff said, he might feel personally that your dad is innocent, but if someone comes in and swears out a warrant or if the circumstantial evidence keeps piling up, he's going to have to make an arrest."

Sylvia nodded. "I've been trying to forget about that," she said, "but I know that it's true."

"The point is," Felicia put in, "what are we going to do about it?"

They thought for a moment.

"As a starter we might go over to see the Bakers," Joan suggested, "and look at the place where the furs were stored. I don't know what we could uncover, but it wouldn't hurt to look around."

They ate an early lunch and went across the hills on their skis.

"If Miss Duncan could only see me now," Joan exclaimed joyously. "Imagine, getting a regular skiing vacation and with her blessing!"

"Don't forget," Felicia reminded her, "that we are going to have to make up all the work we're missing."

The tall girl looked at her reproachfully. "Why

do you have to bring up something like that?" she asked. "And just when I was enjoying myself too."

Sylvia shot ahead, crouching expertly as she sped across the snow. For the time they forgot the real mission they were on. They went down the hill, curved gently to the right, crossed the creek, and started up the opposite slope.

"This isn't nearly as much fun," Felicia said, panting as she made her way up the hill laboriously. "You need a ski lift, Sylvia."

"Remind me before you come the next time, and I'll have one put in for you."

Finally, they reached the Bakers' place. Mrs. Baker came out to greet them.

"It's so good to see you, Sylvia," she said. "And I'm so glad to meet these friends of yours. We heard they had brought you home."

Her husband, Myron, only grunted. He was a squat, dark-visaged man with a perpetual scowl.

"Why, yes," Mrs. Baker said when they told her why they had come. "You can see the place where the furs were stored when they were stolen. Just a minute while I get my coat."

Mr. Baker, who had gone back into the house and sat down, came out with her.

"You can look around out there all you want to," he said, "but you're not going to find anything. The sheriff was out here two or three times, but it must not have done any good. He still hasn't arrested anyone for stealing our furs."

Sylvia reddened slightly at the implication in his voice.

"Now, Myron," his wife scolded, "it doesn't do any good to rake over those things. The sheriff will find the guilty one soon enough."

His scowl darkened. "Not half soon enough to suit me. I lost half a winter's work. That's what I did."

The little shed where they kept their furs was empty, except for a few pelts hanging along the wall.

"What I've caught in the last three weeks," he explained. "Had the place locked up tight, but somebody pried the door open and made off with everything."

"And," Felicia asked, when they had carefully examined the room, "where was the green medallion found?"

His eyes lighted. "The green medallion? How did you know about that?"

"Sheriff Anderson," she said.

"Oh, I had forgotten he would be talking to–" He stopped significantly.

"The medallion was found over in the corner," Mrs. Baker broke in. "The sheriff found it about a week or so after the furs were stolen."

Sylvia Reynolds was biting her lower lip. "I think we had just as well be on our way," she said. "I don't think we'll find anything here."

Mrs. Baker looked at her curiously. "I'm sorry," she said.

Felicia couldn't tell whether she was actually sorry or not.

"We didn't find out a thing," Sylvia said when they were on their way home, "except that Mr. and Mrs. Baker are awfully sure that Dad is the one who stole their furs."

On the hill overlooking the creek, Joan Bailey stopped.

"Look down there," she said, pointing. "Isn't that the same guy we saw yesterday along your dad's trapline?"

Sylvia's throat constricted. For a minute or two, she watched the man lumbering up the creek on snowshoes.

"Why, that's Pierre," she said at last. "Pierre Dufeld."

"He's the guy we met at the general store, isn't he?" Joan asked. "The one who wanted to know when the authorities were going to arrest your dad and put him in jail."

Sylvia nodded. "I don't know why, but he's never liked Dad from the very beginning. They had trouble several years ago. I don't remember what it was about, but I think it had something to do with the trapline. That was before Mom died."

"We know that he talked to you about your dad," Felicia said. "Maybe he has started all these rumors that your dad is the one who has been stealing furs."

"But why?"

"If he wanted to get your dad's trapline, getting

him arrested for stealing would be a sure way of getting it. And starting a lot of stories about him would be a good way of getting people to think that he was guilty."

"You know," Joan broke in, "I think we ought to do a little checking on Mr. Dufeld. If we go over to his place, we might be able to uncover something that would link him to this business."

"What, for instance?" Felicia asked.

Joan shrugged her shoulders. "How would we know until we looked?"

"We–we wouldn't be trespassing, would we?" Felicia asked uneasily.

"Oh, my, no!" Sylvia answered. "His cabin is one that belongs to the government. He just moved into it. We have as much right to go over there and look around as he has to live there."

"All we would have to do is find something that looks suspicious," she continued, "and give the information to Sheriff Anderson. He'd do the rest."

They reached home half an hour before Mr. Reynolds came in. He strode across the clearing on his snowshoes, his rifle in his hand.

"Got something ready for dinner, Sylvia?" he asked as he entered. "I'm about starved."

"It won't be too long. We just got home."

He was getting out of his heavy clothes when there was a sharp knock at the door.

"It's probably for me," he said. "I'll answer it."

Pierre Dufeld was standing in the doorway, his eyes blazing and his lips trembling with rage.

"I was down along the creek just now," he managed angrily, "and somebody shot over my head!"

"Who would do a thing like that?" Sylvia's dad asked. "It was an accident, of course."

"An accident when a man is standing out in the open in broad daylight?" he asked. "An accident when there was nothing else to shoot at?" He took a step closer. "Whoever shoot at Pierre know who he was shooting at. He know it was me!"

"I'm certainly sorry that someone shot at you, Pierre," Mr. Reynolds told him. "Won't you come in and have dinner with us?"

Dufeld's dark face purpled.

"Have dinner?" he echoed. "Have dinner with the man who shoot at me? I would not put my feet under your table if I never get another meal." He turned and spat into the snow contemptuously.

"Now, Pierre," Mr. Reynolds countered, "you don't really believe that I would take a shot at you, do you?"

The French Canadian stared at him for a long minute. "I know you shoot over me!" he said icily. "You make that bullet say, 'Pierre Dufeld, you stay away from my trapline.' But I tell you one thing. As soon as the sheriff throw you in jail, I take over that line of yours. And you are not going to stop me!"

He glared hard at Sylvia's dad, then jerked the door shut and stormed away!

CHAPTER 8

THE ANGRY TRAPPER

That evening, Joan and Felicia had devotions together in their bedroom and sat for a time talking in guarded tones.

"Did you see that look in Pierre Dufeld's eyes?" Joan asked, shuddering at the thought. "He gave me the willies."

"I was just thinking about him," Felicia answered. "He acted to me as though he really had been shot at. He was angry, but he was frightened too. Terribly frightened."

There was a long silence.

"Angry or frightened, I don't want to have trouble with him," Joan repeated. She took a deep breath. "Do you suppose Mr. Reynolds knew Pierre had been fooling around his trapline and shot over his head just to warn him away?"

"It could be, I suppose," Felicia said. "But it doesn't

sound like the other things we know about Sylvia's dad. We know how highly Sheriff Anderson thinks of him and how quickly he insisted on taking the green medallion back to the sheriff. I don't believe that a man like that would shoot over anyone's head deliberately."

She crossed the room and switched out the lights.

"We'll have to keep praying," Joan said at last, "that God will help us to find out the truth."

The next morning Harold Reynolds left the cabin at about the usual time. When he was gone, Sylvia said, "When do you think we ought to go over toward Pierre Dufeld's cabin?"

"Both times we've seen him was in the afternoon," Joan said. "I wonder if he isn't away most every afternoon? We could ski a while this morning and go over there after lunch."

"I almost feel guilty going out and skiing," Sylvia said uneasily. "To think that at any time the sheriff might have to come out here and arrest Dad. When I think about that, I can scarcely stand it."

"We've been praying for him," Felicia reminded her gently, "and for you too, Sylvia."

The Reynolds girl put aside her dish towel and sat down on a chair beside the kitchen table.

"I've tried to pray too," she told them slowly. "I've prayed and prayed and prayed. But it doesn't do any good." Her voice grew cold. "God doesn't even hear. If there is a God!"

"You don't mean that," Felicia said, without raising her voice.

"It depends on how you pray," Joan told her, "and whether you've met the conditions."

"What do you mean, conditions?" Sylvia asked.

The two girls sat down with her and went over the plan of salvation, step by step.

"The Bible says that we 'all have sinned, and come short of the glory of God,'" Felicia said. "But the gift of God is eternal life through Jesus Christ our Lord."

"I still don't know what it means," Sylvia said uneasily.

"It's this way," Joan put in. "The Bible teaches us that none of us is good enough to be saved. That we have all sinned. It also teaches that the wages of sin is death. For that reason, He doesn't expect us to live up to the law in every letter. He knows that we can't. So He has made it possible for us to be saved by our faith. Just by confessing our sin and putting our trust in Jesus Christ to save us."

Sylvia bit her lower lip and ran her hand across her forehead.

"I don't know," she said dismally. "I just don't know."

When the work was done in the little cabin that morning, they went out skiing for an hour or two before lunch. Mr. Reynolds came home to eat and sat in the house for a long while, talking and staring into the fire. It was almost two o'clock before he finally went out again.

"I thought Dad would never go," Sylvia said excitedly. "We're going to have to hurry if we want to get over there and back before dark."

"We could go by car," Joan suggested.

"Oh, that would never do!" the Reynolds girl told her. "His is the only house on that long road. And if he or anyone else even saw the car, they'd know who we were and exactly where we were going."

"That's right too," Joan said.

"And besides," Felicia put in, "we'd much rather ski."

They approached Pierre Dufeld's little cabin stealthily.

"What are we going to do if he's there?" Felicia asked in a hoarse whisper. "What'll we do?"

"Oh, he'll be out somewhere," Sylvia said. "He always is."

Joan shuddered.

"I hope you're right. I can still see that look in his eyes when he came storming up to the cabin yesterday and accused your dad of shooting over him. He's one person I'd hate to have angry with me."

"Now quit talking that way, Joan," Felicia scolded. "If you don't, you'll scare us all."

"If I thought it would, I'd keep right on talking," she whispered, glancing apprehensively over her shoulder.

There was a thin stream of smoke wafting gently upward from the cabin chimney in the still winter air.

"He's home!" Felicia exclaimed, stopping suddenly and grasping Sylvia by the arm.

"No!" the other girl said a moment later. "He's got the fire banked. There would be more smoke than that if he were home and the fire were going well."

"Just the same, I think we ought to be a little careful about how we approach those buildings," she said. "I don't want to have him come charging out with that rifle of his."

They pushed their way over the snow to a place where they could see the buildings through a thin screen of brush.

"I believe you're right," Joan said at last. "I don't see any sign of activity."

They slipped out of their skis and stood them up against one of the log buildings.

"Come over here," Joan said. "I think this must be where he keeps his furs."

The door to the old shed was not locked. She pushed it open.

"Do–do you suppose we ought to go in?" Felicia stammered.

"I don't think there's anything in here," Joan told her. "There's an old pelt hanging on the wall, but it's so badly torn that I don't think it's any good."

The ramshackle old shed did look empty. There

were a few old boards in a far corner, a length of rusty chain, and two or three broken traps.

"I don't think there's anything here at all," Sylvia said. Her voice betrayed her dismay. "We'd better hurry and look at–"

"What's this?" Felicia asked, stooping to pick up a grimy piece of paper.

"Why it looks like a map," Joan said.

Sylvia took it and looked at it intently. "It is a map," she said. "It's a crude one, but I'm sure that it's a map of Dad's trapline."

"Then Pierre Dufeld is interested in getting it away from your father!" Joan exclaimed. "He wasn't kidding yesterday when he made that statement."

"No," Sylvia said, "he wasn't kidding."

At that moment they heard the sound of a vehicle chugging laboriously up the winding trail toward the house.

"Quick!" Sylvia cried. "That's Pierre Dufeld's old car! We've got to get out of here!"

"We don't have time to get to the clearing," Felicia said. "In here!"

The old car was bearing down on them. They ran into the log building.

"What'll we do?" Sylvia asked.

"The only thing we can do," Joan replied, "is to wait right here until after dark. Then we can sneak out and go back to your cabin."

They moved as far into the darkness of the little shed as they could, crouching fearfully.

Felicia began to pray silently, her lips scarcely moving.

Pierre Dufeld drove up in his old car and stopped beside the cabin.

"How long will it be before it gets dark?" Joan whispered.

Sylvia glanced out the half open door at the sky. "It shouldn't be more than an hour."

The time passed endlessly. As night settled down, the cold grew apace. Their bones ached and they shivered in their heavy jackets.

At last darkness came. They greeted it thankfully.

"Are you ready?" Joan whispered.

The other girls nodded.

"Let's go."

They had just reached their skis when they heard a heavy footstep behind them.

"Don't move!" a voice rasped. "Don't move an inch!"

CHAPTER 9

PRISONERS!

The girls stiffened, and, suddenly, Felicia Cartright's blood chilled. A wave of nausea swept over her. She turned slowly, compelled by some strange force within her. She was staring into the short, ugly barrel of a heavy rifle.

"Mr. Dufeld!" she exclaimed, as though his identity had been a surprise to her.

"And who did you expect?" he demanded.

"W-w-we didn't expect anybody," Joan stammered.

"Thought you could come sneaking around here while I wasn't home. First that thieving dad of yours takes my pelts. Then he shoots at me. Now he sends you girls over here to snoop when I'm not home." The rifle was wavering in his hands. "Well, I can tell you that you're not getting away with it. Not for a minute! And if the sheriff can't handle things, I can."

"But we weren't hurting anything," Sylvia managed.

Pierre scarcely heard her. "Thought you could fool me, didn't you? But I knew you were here. I knew it when I first drove up." He laughed mirthlessly.

"We—we were just looking around."

"I know what you were doing," he said. "Now get in the house! All three of you!"

Joan glanced around defiantly.

"Now get in the house," he repeated, motioning with his rifle, "and don't try any funny stuff, or I'll forget my manners."

"You don't have to point that at us," Felicia assured him, her voice trembling. "We won't run away."

"You bet you not run away," he repeated. "If you know what's good for you, you'll go into the cabin quick, like good girls, until Pierre decides what he should do with you. Now be quick. Enough of this talk!"

He herded them into the dirty little cabin. It was only one room and looked as though it hadn't been thoroughly cleaned for years. His bed was in one corner, heaped with dirty, ragged blankets. In the opposite corner was a table and a small kitchen cupboard with the day's dishes, still unwashed, on the counter. The stove was in the middle.

"Now you sit over there," he ordered. "And nothing funny, mind you. I fix up the fire."

* * *

Back in the Reynolds' cabin, Sylvia's father paced the floor anxiously and glanced at his watch. Those girls! They should have been home long ago. He went to the window and looked out.

Sylvia had mentioned something about skiing. Surely if they had gone skiing again, they would not have stayed out after dark. Fear chilled his heart. He knew only too well what could happen in the woods and on skis. One of them could have fallen and broken a leg. They could have gotten lost. They– He pulled out his watch and looked at the time again. Half an hour more and he would go into town and get the sheriff.

He turned on the radio, caught the late news and weather forecast, and waited impatiently. But there was no sign of them. Grimly, he forced his fears aside and got into his heavy coat. If the girls were in trouble, the bitter cold would already be taking its toll. He would have to hurry.

Harold Reynolds drove as fast as he dared over the snow-packed road to the sheriff's house in Morrisville.

"I don't like to bother you this way, Ed," he said uneasily, "but they should have been home hours ago. I'm afraid they're lost or that one of them got hurt."

"I don't blame you at all, Harold," the officer said. "Do you know where the girls were going or what they planned to do?"

Sylvia's dad shook his head.

The sheriff went to the phone.

"I'll get a couple of my deputies, Harold," he said, "and we'll go out and see if we can find them. Sylvia was along, wasn't she?"

"Oh, yes!"

"Then she ought not to be lost. She knows these woods as well as you and I do."

"I know that," Harold replied, "but there's something else that's bothering me. Those girls have been terribly interested in this trouble I've been having. They might have fooled around and stumbled onto something that has gotten them into trouble."

Sheriff Anderson looked at him quizzically. "Could be," he said. "At any rate, we'll soon know."

* * *

Pierre Dufeld built up the fire in the little wood stove and sat down in a chair across from the girls. His hunting rifle lay across his lap in easy reach.

"Now you sit there and make no trouble for Pierre," he said warningly. "Then there be no trouble for you." He paused. "No more trouble than you've already got, that is."

"But what are you going to do with us?" Joan asked him. "You–you just can't keep us here indefinitely."

"That," he announced, his voice firm, "is for Pierre Dufeld to decide." He leaned back in the chair and squinted at them. "The next time you try to fool someone, you be sure that it is not someone like Pierre. You have real trouble."

The girls did not speak for a long while. They sat there uncomfortably, looking at one another and at their angry captor.

"What do you suppose he's going to do with us?" Sylvia whispered. "I–I'm scared."

"So am I," Joan said under her breath.

Felicia Cartright closed her eyes and began to pray. "Our Father and our God," she prayed softly, her words scarcely audible, "we come to You now, praying for guidance and help. You know everything, and You direct our paths. We're so weak and frightened. We don't know what to do. Be with us, Lord. We pray that You would soften Pierre's heart so that he will let us go. Or help us to–to get away. And be with Mr. Reynolds and help him not to worry about us. And, O Lord, help us to find out who has stolen the furs, so people won't suspect Sylvia's dad anymore. In Jesus's name, Amen."

Sylvia Reynolds looked up at her wistfully.

"I–I'd give anything in the world to be able to pray that way," she said after a time.

Felicia glanced at Pierre. If he was listening, he gave no sign. He sat there motionless, his eyes never leaving them.

"There is something that is more important than even being able to pray," the Christian girl went on. "In fact, it comes before prayer."

"And what's that?" Sylvia asked hungrily.

"That is to know that you're right with God. And to know that whatever happens, you are safe in His care."

Sylvia's eyes widened. "But can you know that?" she asked doubtfully. "Can you be saved and really know it *now*?" she asked.

Felicia nodded firmly.

"You can be saved and know it now," she said. "The very minute that you trust Christ as your personal Savior. "'But as many as received him, to them gave he power to become the sons of God,'" she quoted, "'even to them that believe on his name.'"

"That was one thing that bothered me at first," Joan put in. "When I first began to think seriously about spiritual things, I wondered how a person could be saved and know it. But I've found now that it's true. That's one of the glorious things about salvation. You can enjoy it now. Right from the very beginning."

For a long while, Sylvia sat there silently, breathing heavily.

"Now would be a good time to get the whole affair straightened out," Felicia continued. "You are concerned about your soul. I can see that in your eyes. You want to confess your sin and put it under the blood of Christ. What's holding you back, Sylvia? Why don't you turn your life over to Jesus Christ?"

Sylvia Reynolds swallowed hard and bit her lower lip.

"I–I'm not sure I understand it all," she said, "or that I could live up to it."

"If you really mean business with the Lord," Joan said, "you can put your trust in Him to help you live the way a Christian ought to live."

"That's exactly right," the Cartright girl added. "A Christian can no more live up to a Christian life himself than he could live up to the law before he accepted Christ as his Savior. If we had to do that, then none of us could be Christians. But God doesn't expect us to do it alone. He doesn't even want us to try because He knows that we'll fail. All we have to do is to confess our sins and put our trust in Him to save us and to help us to live as we should."

The clock on the wall struck three.

When it was finished, Sylvia turned to her companions.

"Would you pray with me?" she asked, her voice hoarse.

The three of them bowed their heads together. Sylvia prayed first, haltingly. Then Joan, and finally Felicia prayed, thanking God for bringing their friend to a saving knowledge of Himself and asking Him to help her to live a good Christian life. When they finished, Sylvia looked around uncertainly.

"I don't feel any differently," she said at last. "Am I supposed to?"

"Feeling doesn't have a thing to do with it," Felicia assured her. "That will come later, after you've been reading your Bible and praying and being part of a church. Feeling will grow as time passes. Right now, you've taken the most important step. The other things will come later."

"You know," Sylvia said, "I'm glad this is over. I

kept feeling that I was going to take a stand for Christ almost from the first time you girls started talking with me. But I kept putting it off. I think I was afraid to let the Lord Jesus have control of my life."

The three girls slept a little, fitfully, after a time. Felicia heard the clock strike five and six. She roused a little and glanced across the room. The lamp had been turned low, and the fire was almost out. Pierre Dufeld was slouched in the chair. If only – He was! Her heart soared! He was asleep!

Tensely, the Cartright girl reached over and touched Joan and Sylvia. Joan groaned protestingly, and Felicia put her hand over her mouth in warning. At last, the three of them were awake.

Felicia motioned significantly toward the door and their coats that Pierre had thrown carelessly in a pile on the floor. They dared not risk talking, even in whispers.

With a prayer in their hearts, they got silently to their feet and tiptoed across the floor.

The old trapper did not move.

Felicia opened the door cautiously after wriggling into her coat, and the other two inched out.

"Now to get those skis," Joan whispered.

As Felicia followed them out into penetrating cold, her foot slipped, and the heavy storm door jerked out of her hand. The spring slammed it shut!

Pierre Dufeld leaped to his feet with a start!

"Come back here!" he shouted in desperation. "Come back, or I'll shoot!"

CHAPTER 10

THE GIRLS ESCAPE

"This way!" Joan cried, pushing frantically through the deep snow toward the brush at the edge of the clearing. "Hurry!"

Pierre Dufeld must have stood for a moment, sleepily, before stumbling to the door. They had almost reached the edge of the clearing when he threw open the door.

"You, out there!" he shouted, clutching his rifle menacingly. "I see you! Come back here! Come back, or I'll shoot!"

They ran into the brush.

"If he follows us, we're done for!" Sylvia cried. "He can put on a pair of snowshoes and follow us wherever we go and twice as fast as we can run in this snow."

"Not if we get those skis," Joan retorted.

The girls glanced at one another in the darkness.

"But where are they?" Felicia asked. "What did he do with them?"

"They're up by the cabin door," the Reynolds girl said, her voice weak. "Don't you remember?"

The silence grew around them. Felicia started to speak but could not.

"Now what are we going to do?" Joan Bailey asked. "Go back around the road? It would be a great deal farther that way, but we would have a path to walk in."

"Let's wait and see what he does," Felicia said. "Maybe we can sneak back and get our skis."

"You always think of such pleasant things," Joan told her.

The girls prayed together and then crouched, shivering, in the brush.

"I–I don't believe that he is going to follow us," Sylvia managed at last, "or he'd have come out after us right away before we had a chance to get too far."

"Maybe he's sitting inside waiting for us to come back for our skis," Joan said, "the way he waited for us to come out of the shed last night."

Felicia caught her breath. "I hadn't thought of that."

"We had just as well start walking around the road."

But before they could move, the cabin door opened and Pierre Dufeld came out, buttoning his heavy coat as he went.

"Now we are in for it," Sylvia muttered softly.

Joan put her hand up, warningly, to her lips.

Instead of following them into the brush, Pierre

went around the cabin. A moment later they heard the whine of the starter and the asthmatic cough of his old car.

"He thinks we've walked along the road," Joan said exultantly. "He's going after us in his car.

They sprawled breathlessly in the snow as the car lights swung over them and headed up the lane. As soon as the car disappeared, Joan got to her feet and began to brush the snow off her clothes. The others did the same.

"We're going to have to hurry," Felicia said. "He may only go half a mile or so and realize that we didn't go out on the road after all. We can't have him catch us this time."

They hurried back to the cabin and got their skis.

"It's a good thing he didn't think of breaking these or putting them away somewhere," Sylvia said as they fastened the straps. "If he had, we'd be done for."

Once on the skis, they made their way clumsily out of the clearing and started down the long, gentle slope.

"Mr. Dufeld was even angrier when he found us at his place than he was when he came over to the cabin and accused your dad of shooting at him," Joan said after a time. "Why do you suppose he got so mad?"

"I think it must have been because he was afraid that we'd find something that would link him to those fur robberies," Sylvia said. "He didn't even give us a chance to explain."

"I suppose we shouldn't have gone over to his place," Felicia said.

"But we didn't hurt anything. All we were doing was looking around," Sylvia continued.

"And found nothing," Joan added, laconically.

"Oh, we found out one thing!" Felicia answered. "We already had an inkling that Mr. Dufeld was interested in your dad's trapline. But now that we found that map we know for sure."

"Just the same," Joan said, shuddering, "I'm going to give that place a wide berth from now on. I don't want to have any more trouble with Pierre Dufeld if I can help it."

"Do you suppose he'll come back to his cabin when he doesn't find us along the road and follow after us?" Sylvia asked.

Felicia glanced over her shoulder. "There isn't any sign of him back there, but I don't care to wait around to find out."

When they reached the Reynolds' cabin, Sylvia's dad came out to meet them.

"Sylvia!" he cried. "Where have you been? We've been looking all over for you."

"We knew you'd be terribly worried," she said, telling him quickly what had happened. "But there wasn't a thing we could do about it."

"I thought we ought to go over to Pierre's and have a look," Mr. Reynolds said, "but Sheriff Anderson was so sure that it would be a waste of time." His face grew stern. "You girls shouldn't have gone over to his cabin. You know that, don't you?"

"We know better than to try it again," Joan said with considerable feeling.

Harold Reynolds straightened suddenly. "I've got to get hold of Ed right away. He was going to call the sheriff at Hammond and have him bring over his bloodhounds to follow you." He started for his coat. "I came home to get some of your clothes to let the bloodhounds sniff. We thought you were lost or had fallen while skiing. I don't mind telling you we've put in an awful night."

"It wasn't so much fun for us either," the Bailey girl answered. "We were sitting in that old trapper's cabin, looking down the barrel of his hunting rifle."

"You shouldn't have gone over to Dufeld's place," Mr. Reynolds said again. "You know what a violent temper he has. It's a wonder you got off as easily as you did."

"But, Dad," Sylvia protested, "we can't let them arrest you and send you to jail without doing something! And that's what's going to happen unless we can get some evidence that you didn't steal those furs."

For a long minute he stared off into space.

"I don't know," he said after a long time, wearily, as though all the strength had drained out of him. "It doesn't seem as though anything we can do will change that."

They were still standing in the cabin talking

when a car drove into the yard and the sheriff and two men got out.

Felicia went to the window and looked out.

"Why, it's Pierre!" she exclaimed fearfully. "And Mr. Baker with Sheriff Anderson! I wonder what they want!"

Harold Reynolds went to answer the imperious knock at the door. As he opened it, the burly trapper pushed him aside and went storming into the cabin.

"Where are they?" he demanded, his voice quivering with rage. And then he saw the girls. "I told you that you couldn't get away from Pierre Dufeld! I warned you!"

"You'd better let me handle this, Pierre," the sheriff broke in.

"That's why I brought you along," he stormed. "So you would handle it. They broke into my place! I want them punished!"

"Now just a minute, Dufeld," Harold Reynolds cut in. "Did the girls actually break into your cabin? Hadn't they only approached your place and looked into that old shed you haven't used for years?"

"Just the same I don't like the idea of having anyone come over to my place snooping around. When the girls sneaked away from me, I went over to Myron's. And he and I decided that the thing to do was to get the sheriff and have a showdown."

"We are terribly sorry that we went over to your

place and bothered you," Felicia said. "We just didn't think."

"You're going to have a long time to think about it when I get through with you," the angry trapper rasped. "First my furs are stolen. Then somebody shoots over my head and I'm not doing anything. Now I find you breaking into my place, trying to see if I have anything else that is worth stealing."

"We've been too easy on them," Myron Baker broke in. "They were over at our place snooping around. Now they go to your place. Do you know what they're trying to do, Pierre? They're trying to fix the blame of those fur robberies on one of us! That's what they're after! Are we going to let them get away with it?"

"They've got away with too much already," Pierre retorted. "I'm going to see that they don't get away with this."

"Just a minute, Pierre," the sheriff broke in. "It seems that I remember something about that place of yours. Actually, it's on government land. You just moved into the cabin and squatted there without buying it or paying rent or taxes or anything. Actually, you're trespassing over there just as much as they were. More so because you've taken over."

Pierre Dufeld's face flushed. "I–I guess I wasn't using that old shed they went in," he acknowledged. "And they didn't make any attempt to get into the cabin or the shed I had locked."

"Actually, we wouldn't even have gone into it if we hadn't heard you coming and gotten frightened," Felicia explained.

The trapper turned back to the sheriff. "Maybe they didn't break into my place. Maybe I can't do anything about that, but I did catch that silver-cross fox Harold Reynolds made into a fur piece for this girl of his."

"Are you sure of that, Pierre?" the sheriff asked him. "Are you positive that you can identify the fur?"

Pierre Dufeld drew himself up haughtily. "If you will make her bring it out, I show you I can identify it!"

CHAPTER II

THE SILVER-CROSS FUR PIECE

That's a harsh accusation, Pierre," the sheriff said. "Just the same," he went on hotly, "I know that fur. I catch him myself."

Harold Reynolds turned to Sylvia. "Go and get your fur piece, my dear," he said.

"Perhaps you had better describe it first, Dufeld," the sheriff said. "That will make for a more positive identification."

He was silent for a moment.

"The fur shines," he said at last, "with a luster you have never seen on another silver-cross. He was a big fox. Marked in this manner." Pierre took a stubby pencil from his pocket and made a rough outline on a scrap of paper.

Sylvia brought the fur piece, and Dufeld took it in his hands.

"See!" he exclaimed. "Look at the beauty of the

fur! Look how it shines! There has never been another silver-cross taken in these parts for the last ten years that is half so beautiful."

"It is a beautiful fur," the sheriff said, examining it carefully. "But you saw this on Sylvia. You could have remembered the markings. Is there anything else that makes it distinctive?"

Pierre turned to his trapper companion.

"You were there, Myron!" he exclaimed heatedly. "You saw it with your eyes right after I took it from the trap. Remember what you said? That it was the most beautiful silver-cross you had ever seen come from around here!" He held the fur piece in his hand. "This is mine! I swear it!"

"It certainly looks like the fur you took, Pierre," Myron Baker said, examining the fur again. "In fact, I'm convinced that it's yours. Yes, this is the same silver-cross fox that I saw you take from your trap."

Sheriff Anderson turned slowly to Sylvia's dad. "What do you have to say to that, Harold?" he asked.

"What can I say except that they are mistaken," Mr. Reynolds said. "I took that fur myself, and I made it up into a neckpiece for Sylvia. That's all I can tell you."

Felicia stepped forward quickly. "Did I understand you to say that you had tanned this fur yourself, Mr. Dufeld?" she asked. "Before it was stolen, I mean."

"Positively. It was so beautiful a fur that I plan to keep it for myself."

"And how did you tan it?" she insisted.

"The same way I always tan," Pierre retorted brusquely. "Why? What are you talking about?"

"You don't have to answer her questions, Pierre," Baker told him. "You've identified the fur. That's all that matters."

"I would like to show you something." She took a razor blade from the window ledge and cut the threads that held the lining in place. "Feel this. Do you tan hides as soft as this?"

He rubbed it speculatively between his thumb and forefinger.

"Pierre does as nice a job of tanning as anyone else in this part of Maine," Myron Baker explained. "I'd vouch for that. And so will anyone else who knows anything about it. I don't know what you're trying to prove, young lady, but I can tell you now that it isn't going to work. This fur piece belongs to Pierre. I'd swear it."

"Answer her question, Pierre," Sheriff Anderson said softly.

"Yes," the trapper replied, "I–I think I tan so soft. I give special care to it."

"But you tanned it the same way you always do," she repeated, "the–the commercial way. Is that right?"

"That's what I tell you, isn't it?"

"I don't know what all this has got to do with it," Baker demanded. "I'm sleepy. I want to get back home as soon as this mess is cleaned up."

"I want to show you something about this fur, Sheriff Anderson," Felicia said. "Smell it. Wasn't it tanned with smoke?"

The sheriff held the fur piece to his nose and sniffed it. "It does have a smoky odor at that. But I don't see–

"I just remembered what Sylvia told us about the way her dad tanned hides," she went on breathlessly. "She said that he learned from the Native Americans that using smoke and some other preparations gave a softer, more durable hide. So this smell of smoke and the smoky color to the hide proves that Mr. Reynolds actually tanned this pelt."

A strange, perplexed look came across Pierre's face.

"He could have smoked it a little after he stole it," Myron Baker put in. "That doesn't prove anything. They're just trying to get out of it. And it looks to me as though you're doing everything you can to help them, Sheriff."

"I don't want to see an innocent man arrested," the officer said. "Pierre hasn't been able to make a positive identification that the fur was his."

"You forget about my testimony. And another thing. How many silver-cross foxes do you think are taken up here every season? You've lived here a long while. You know that one a year is just about the limit. That's evidence in itself." He drew himself up haughtily. "Are you going to take Harold Reynolds in or aren't you?"

Joan turned to Mr. Baker.

"Didn't we see a silver-cross pelt over at your place the other day?" she asked innocently.

For a brief instant he glared at her.

"Yes," he retorted. "I did catch a silver-cross. And if anyone wants to doubt that I got it myself, I can furnish ample proof that I caught it." He turned back to the sheriff. "How long do we have to put up with this sort of thing?" he demanded. "You've got a mountain of evidence. What more do you want?"

"That is right!" Pierre snarled menacingly. "I am shot at and robbed. Are you going to arrest him or aren't you?"

Before Sheriff Anderson could speak, Felicia moved closer to Mr. Baker. "But none of those things are evidence," she protested heatedly. "They aren't evidence at all, and you know it."

"They are evidence enough for Pierre and for me," he told her.

"But it isn't the sort of evidence that will stand up in court, is it, Mr. Baker?" Her voice rose as she spoke. Sylvia and Joan stared at her curiously. "This is all circumstantial evidence. A judge might throw it all out and leave the prosecution without a thing to prove its case."

The color came up into his neck, and perspiration dotted his forehead. "I think the evidence is strong enough," he said. "It is enough to prove Reynolds' guilt to me."

"Name just one piece of evidence that points to Mr. Reynolds," Felicia persisted. "Show me just one thing!"

Sheriff Anderson started to protest, but the look in her eyes held him momentarily.

"If the sheriff would search this cabin, he'd find the evidence," Baker answered heatedly.

"What evidence?" She lashed the question out suddenly, belligerently.

"The green medallion, for one thing." He spoke before he thought.

"What about the medallion?" she asked quickly. "How would that prove anything?"

Myron Baker lost his temper. "Harold Reynolds always carried it in his pocket," he snapped, "until he lost it over at my place when he stole my furs. It was stolen from the sheriff's office day before yesterday. That green medallion is one thing that Harold Reynolds can't lie out of."

Sheriff Anderson stiffened and glanced over at Harold Reynolds.

"I don't see how that proves Sylvia's dad is guilty," Felicia continued.

"When they find it on him, it'll prove plenty," Myron Baker told her. "The trouble is that nobody has looked for it around here!"

With that he stormed out onto the porch and made for the jacket that was still hanging there. "When you find that medallion here, you'll know who's guilty!"

Sheriff Anderson was right beside him.

"Baker," he said icily, "you have a great deal of explaining to do!"

CHAPTER 12

GIRL "SHERLOCK HOLMES"

Myron Baker froze where he was, his hand half in the pocket of the jacket on the porch.

"W-w-what do you mean?" he asked lamely. "I was just tired of waiting for you to do something about pinning this fur stealing on Harold Reynolds. That's all. So I decided to do some looking for myself." He turned around. "Of course, if you want to make your own investigation–"

"I don't think it will be necessary to make an investigation," the sheriff said, "thanks to this young lady." He turned to Felicia. "I was going to stop you, Miss Cartright," he said, "but then I realized what you were trying to do, and I thought it was worth a chance. I guess it was too."

"What do you mean?" Myron Baker demanded angrily. "What kind of talk is that?"

Sheriff Anderson guided them back into the cabin and closed the door.

"You gave yourself away just now, Baker. I think you'd better sit down and give us the whole story."

"I gave myself away?" he blustered. "What are you trying to do? Be funny and try to pin this thing on me?"

The officer shook his head. "You've already taken care of that, very neatly."

The girls looked at one another happily.

Sheriff Anderson took the green medallion from his pocket and showed it to Baker.

"Harold Reynolds found this in his jacket pocket and brought it to me," he explained. "I said nothing to anyone that would let them know the medallion was the thing that was stolen from my office. I asked Harold and the girls to say nothing to anyone about it."

"So–?" Baker was glaring at him.

"The only other person who knew about it was the person who stole it from me and planted it out here."

"So you're the one who has been stealing those furs!" Harold Reynolds exclaimed. "I would never have guessed it!"

Baker did not answer.

"I should have suspected you a long while ago, Myron," Ed Anderson continued. "You're the one who came to me at first and said you wanted me to arrest Harold for stealing your furs. I should have known you had some reason for wanting to get me after Reynolds."

"But why?" Sylvia's dad broke in. "Myron and I have never had trouble."

"No," Sheriff Anderson replied, "but you have the best trapline in this part of Maine. And you are always bringing in more pelts than the others. He wanted your trapline. That's what he wanted."

"And I'd have gotten it too," Baker said, "if it hadn't been for that girl."

Pierre Dufeld had been standing there silently, turning the matter over in his mind.

"So that's what you were doing when you keep telling Pierre that Reynolds steal his furs," the trapper said. "You want me to help you so you can get his trapline." He pursed his lips. "Then you must be the one who shot at me when I was looking over the territory."

"You didn't think I was going to let you take over after I'd gone to all that trouble, did you?" Baker demanded.

"And that silver-cross pelt the girls saw at your place," Pierre continued, "that's mine!"

"Yes," Myron Baker snarled, "that pelt's yours! Now I've told you everything I'm going to."

"I think you've told us everything that's necessary," Sheriff Anderson replied. "Get your coat, Baker. You and I are going to town."

Harold Reynolds came up to Pierre and held out

his hand. "Pierre," he said, "I owe you an apology. I must admit that I thought you were the one who had been stealing the furs and were trying to blame me for it."

"I have been wrong too," the old trapper said. "I am sorry for holding the girls at my cabin. I knew they had done nothing, but I was so furious because the sheriff hadn't arrested you and got my pelts back."

Sheriff Anderson started out the door with his prisoner. "I'll send a deputy out to pick up your silver fox pelt, Pierre," he said, "and make a complete search of the farm. I think we'll be able to turn up the rest of the pelts without trouble."

"Thank you, Sheriff," Pierre said gratefully. "And thank you, young lady. You help keep Pierre from making a terrible mistake."

No one said any more until after the sheriff and Myron Baker were gone.

"I will go now, Reynolds." The burly trapper started out the door.

"Just a minute and I'll drive you home."

When they were gone, Joan and Sylvia turned to the Cartright girl excitedly.

"Oh, Felicia!" Sylvia exclaimed. "That was wonderful! What made you suspect Mr. Baker? I was so sure that Pierre was the guilty one.

"I'm not just sure," she said sitting down. "It seemed strange to me that he kept breaking in when

Pierre was talking, as though he wanted to get your dad arrested right away."

"I believe that's the first time I ever saw you angry," Joan observed. "I didn't even know that you could raise your voice. I surely wouldn't want to have trouble with you after an exhibition like that."

Felicia laughed.

"I had to make him angry," she said. "Angry enough to lose his head and betray himself. I was positive that he was the one who had stolen the green medallion from your dad and planted it over at his place so the sheriff would find it. You remember it wasn't found on the first visit of the sheriff. It was found sometime later. That seemed suspicious to me. Then, when the officer still didn't arrest your father, Baker got desperate and stole it from the sheriff's office and planted it out here. He must have figured that your dad wouldn't find it until he got the sheriff over here to search the place, or if he did, that he'd keep it around."

"To think that I room with a detective," Joan said cheerily. "I'm going to have to give up my life of crime or 'Sherlock Holmes' Cartright will gather the evidence and throw me behind bars."

They were silent then and sat looking at one another.

"I feel as though I've had a terrible weight lifted from my shoulders," Sylvia said at last, her voice hushed. "You'll never know how awful it is to have your father blamed for something like that."

"We can thank God that he was proved innocent," Felicia said. "I'm sure it was in answer to our prayers."

Sylvia got up and crossed the room.

"I have you to thank that I found Christ as my Savior too. That really has been the most wonderful thing of all."

Joan and Felicia both smiled happily.

* * *

"Well," Felicia said the following morning as they got their bags into the car and made ready to go back to Wellington, "do you think Miss Duncan will be surprised when you go back with us?"

Sylvia shook her head, smiling warmly. "Dad called her yesterday afternoon and explained everything," she said. "He also explained why you've been delayed, so you won't get into any trouble."

"Did he talk her out of making up our work?" Joan asked.

Sylvia shook her head. "I'm afraid not."

"That would be too good to be true," she said laconically. "Of course, I haven't told you and Felicia yet, but there is a fee for riding back to Wellington with me. You are each going to have to do my homework in one subject. That ought to be fair enough, hadn't it?"

"Oh, but you forget something!" Sylvia countered. "Felicia's the detective. She'd find out you didn't do your homework yourself, and then you would be in trouble."

"And I'd turn you in too," she laughed.

"A fine roommate you turned out to be," Joan retorted. "Get in and let's be on our way before I change my mind."

Mr. Reynolds was standing in the cabin door waving to them as they pulled out of the yard.

THE
FELICIA CARTRIGHT
SERIES

Felicia Cartright, a petite blonde who is one of the most popular students at Wellington School for Girls, has a surprising inclination toward mysteries. If a mysterious situation arises, it either makes its way to Felicia, or Felicia somehow finds it. Though this is a bit trying for her happy-go-lucky roommate, Joan Bailey, it does prevent life from becoming monotonous. It also enables Bernard Palmer, the popular author of the "Danny Orlis" books, to write an entertaining series of stories for girls aged twelve to eighteen.

The mysteries range from a valuable missing antique to an attempt by claim jumpers to steal a deposit of tungsten ore. There's excitement and action galore—but there's also spiritual guidance and blessing because Felicia and her partner-in-adventure love the Lord and take Him into account in all their experiences.

AVAILABLE FROM WWW.ANEKOPRESS.COM